An Animal Family

DEER AND FAWNS

By Shep Fields

Gareth Stevens
PUBLISHING

Please visit our website, www.garethstevens.com. For a free color catalog of all our high-quality books, call toll free 1-800-542-2595 or fax 1-877-542-2596.

Cataloging-in-Publication Data
Names: Fields, Shep.
Title: Deer and fawns / Shep Fields.
Description: New York : Gareth Stevens Publishing, 2018. | Series: An animal family | Includes index.
Identifiers: ISBN 9781482463736 (pbk.) | ISBN 9781482463750 (library bound) | ISBN 9781482463743 (6 pack)
Subjects: LCSH: Deer–Juvenile literature. | Fawns–Juvenile literature.
Classification: LCC QL737.U55 F54 2018 | DDC 599.65–dc23

First Edition

Published in 2018 by
Gareth Stevens Publishing
111 East 14th Street, Suite 349
New York, NY 10003

Editor: Ryan Nagelhout
Designer: Samantha DeMartin

Photo credits: Cover, p.1 Holly Kuchera/Shutterstock.com; p. 5 Volodymyr Burdiak/Shutterstock.com; p. 7 (top left) Matt Gibson/Shutterstock.com; p. 7 (bottom left) davemhuntphotography/Shutterstock.com; p. 7 (bottom right) EcoPrint/Shutterstock.com; p. 7 (top right) Alexey Seafarer/Shutterstock.com; p. 9 Matt Gibson/Shutterstock.com; p. 11 Ms. K/Shutterstock.com; p. 13 Giedriius/Shutterstock.com; pp. 15, 24 (fawn) SniperSteve/Shutterstock.com; p. 17 Mark Caunt/Shutterstock.com; pp. 19, 24 Betty Shelton/Shutterstock.com; p. 21 Jeffery B. Banke/Shutterstock.com; p. 23 Warren Price Photography/Shutterstock.com.

Printed in the United States of America

CPSIA compliance information: Batch #CS17GS: For further information contact Gareth Stevens, New York, New York at 1-800-542-2595.

Contents

Deer love to run.
They are very fast.

There are more than 100 kinds.

Some deer live
in the forest.

They eat lots of plants.

Deer love to eat leaves.

Baby deer are
called fawns.
They are very cute.

Most deer are brown.
They have lots of fur.

Fawns have white spots. The spots keep them safe.

The spots go away
as they grow.

Mother deer keep babies safe, too. They stay close to fawns.

Words to Know

fawn

spot

Index